Lóng is a Dragon

Chinese Writing
for Children

by Peggy Goldstein

PACIFIC VIEW PRESS
BERKELEY, CALIFORNIA

About the Author:

Peggy Goldstein is an American sculptor, printmaker and designer whose works have been exhibited in North and South America and Europe, and have been awarded numerous prizes. She is represented in museums, national libraries and private collections in Canada, the United States, the United Kingdom, France and Switzerland. Ms. Goldstein has studied Chinese calligraphy under Ung No Lee at the Academie de Peinture Orientale in Paris, and has taught at the Smithsonian Institution's Anacostia Neighborhood Museum and at the American College in Paris. She currently lives in France.

Text, illustrations, and calligraphy by Peggy R. Goldstein
Cover illustration by Jos Sances
Cover design by Rob Hugel
Book design by Linda Revel

Library of Congress Cataloging-in-Publication Data
The Library of Congress has catalogued the original edition as follows:

Goldstein, Peggy, 1921–
        Lóng is a dragon in Chinese / by Peggy Goldstein.
            p.   cm.
        Summary: Explains how Chinese writing developed and demonstrates how to write seventy-five Chinese characters, using detailed instructions and examples.
            ISBN 0-8351-2375-8 : $14.95
            1. Chinese language—Writing—Juvenile literature.   (Chinese language—Writing.)
I. Title
PL1171.G65   1990
495.1'1—dc20   90-81148
                                                                                       CIP
                                                                                        AC

ISBN 1-881896-01-3 : $15.95

Printed in the United States of America by **Pacific View Press.**

Long, long ago, before

before

even before

no one knew how to read or write!

Then people in China saw that footprints in the mud were **signs** showing who had been there. So they took sticks and scratched in the mud. They made pictures of important things.

Other people saw and understood the signs because they looked like real things. Soon many people could read and write them. Here are some of the early signs.

The sign for **sun** was a circle with a wavy line through it to show heat waves.

sun

The **moon** showed a crescent or half-moon.

moon

The sign for **mountain** had three peaks.

mountain

Rain showed drops falling from the sky.

rain

The **child** was reaching for mother.

child

Woman showed an active, busy person.

woman

Fire blazed from burning wood.

fire

Cart was a box between two wheels.

cart

These were the signs of ancient times, more than 5000 years ago. They were carved into bamboo and clay pots and bones, and they were cast into metal.

After inventing brushes and pens people could draw the signs in a different way. Today they are called **characters** and are written like this:

sun

moon

mountain

rain

child

woman

fire

cart

Many Chinese characters represent animals. Chinese folklore is a rich storehouse of animal stories and legends.

The illustrations here show how ancient signs have come from animal shapes and how the characters are written today.

	ancient	**current**

ox

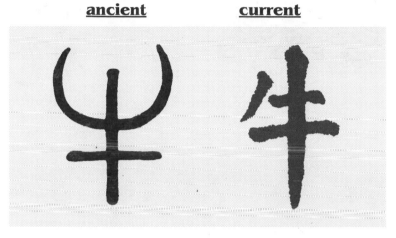

sheep

insect

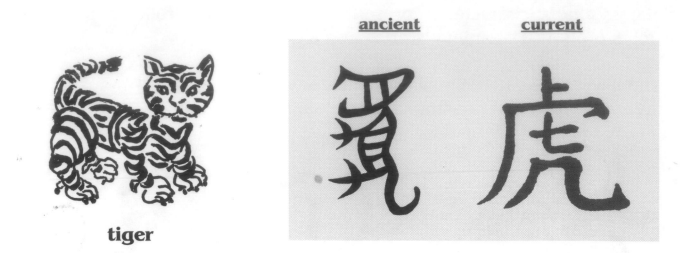

ancient   current

tiger

bird

horse

rat

tortoise

deer

ancient   **current**

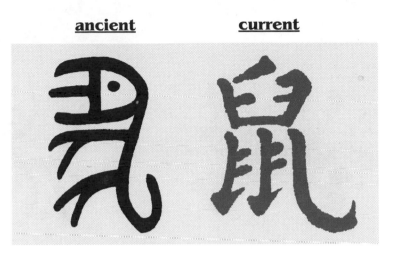

dog

fish

dragon

Called **lóng** in Chinese, the **dragon** is a symbol of strength and kindness, a source of protection and help for all people.

Before you start to write Chinese characters, you need to know that each part of a character is called a **stroke**. Practice copying these basic strokes a few times before you start to write the characters shown on the following pages. These are the basic strokes for Chinese writing. Draw all the vertical strokes from the top down and the horizontal ones from left to right, as the **arrows** show.

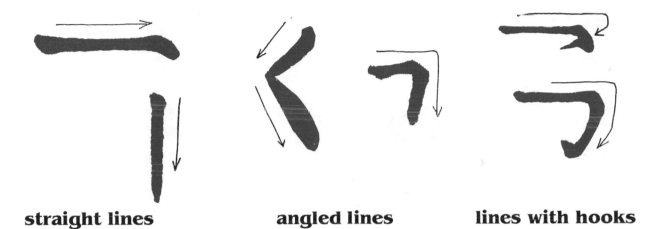

straight lines   **angled lines**   **lines with hooks**

Curves also move from top to bottom and from left to right.

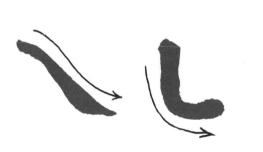

curves   **curves with hooks**

Some short strokes slant left, and some slant to the right.

short strokes

Only 1 stroke is written from the bottom up,

as in these characters:

water   **ice**

and only one from right to left, as in the character for **tongue**:

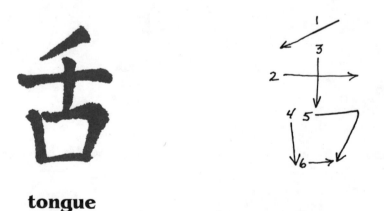

tongue

You are now ready to begin writing Chinese characters.

Always draw the strokes in the direction shown by the arrows.

Always draw them in the **order** in which the arrows are **numbered**.

How well can you write these Chinese characters?

 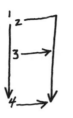

sun

moon

mountain

rain

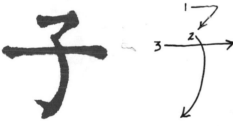

child

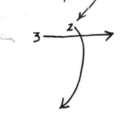

woman

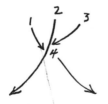

fire

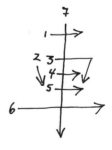

cart

Now you know how to write 8 Chinese characters. You will also want to know how the words sound in Chinese. To show you how to **pronounce** them, they are written here using our alphabet. When pronounced in Chinese, **x** sounds like **sh—** and **q** like **ch—**. For example, **xia** is "shia" and **qing** is "ching."

Chinese is a musical language. There are four **tones** in official spoken Chinese, also called Mandarin. The tones are shown by the little marks over the vowels: level (–), rising (é), falling-and-rising (ˇ), and falling (`). The meaning of a word changes when its tone changes.

Write the characters again and pronounce them in Chinese when you do. This will help you remember how to write them.

sun, rì   **moon, yuè**   **mountain, shān**   **rain, yǔ**

woman, nǚ   **child, zǐ**   **fire, huǒ**   **cart, chē**

The characters for animals that you met on pages 5, 6, 7 and 8 are shown here with correct stroke order and Chinese pronunciation.

Practice writing them.

Now you are ready to **count** in Chinese.

one yī

two èr

three sān

four sì

five wŭ

six liù

seven qī

eight bā

nine jiŭ

ten shí

eleven shí yī

twelve shí èr

Diăn is o'clock or hour in Chinese.

What time is it?

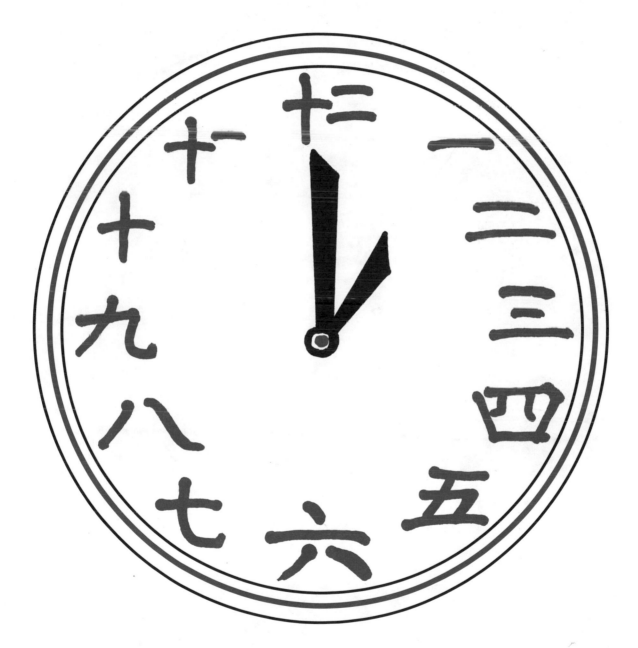

What time will it be in two hours from now? In three hours? Five?

Notice that the page numbers in this book are also in Chinese.

Count while you write the **numbers**. Pronounce each number as you write.

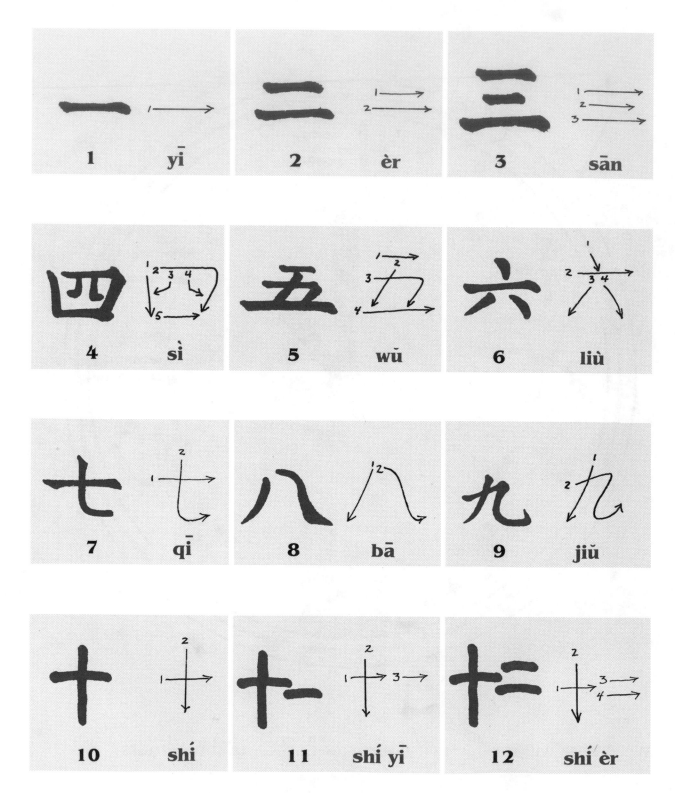

1 yī	**2** èr	**3** sān
4 sì	**5** wǔ	**6** liù
7 qī	**8** bā	**9** jiǔ
10 shí	**11** shí yī	**12** shí èr

You have seen how to write **12** numbers, **12** animals, and **8** characters that developed from pictures.

Here are **6** more characters that look like what they mean:

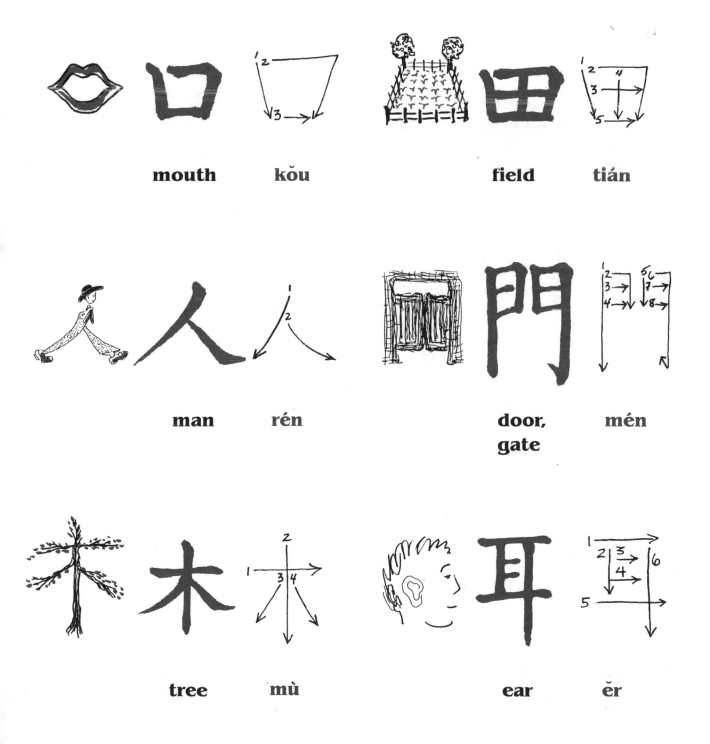

| mouth | kǒu | | field | tián |

| man | rén | | door, gate | mén |

| tree | mù | | ear | ěr |

You know that many characters represent **things**:

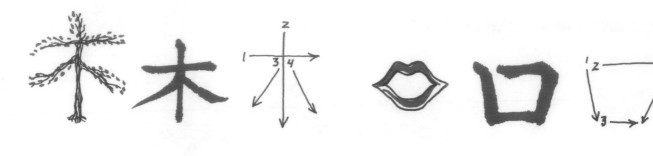

tree   **mù**   **mouth**   **kǒu**

Others express **ideas**:

 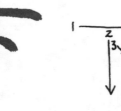

down   **xià**   **up**   **shàng**

Still others express **actions**:

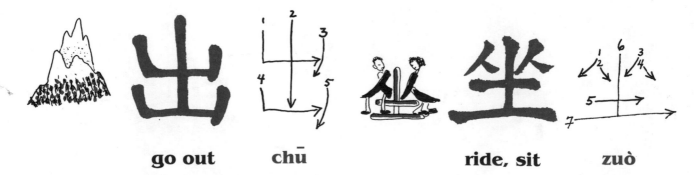

go out   **chū**   **ride, sit**   **zuò**

The character for **go out** looks like a mountain "growing" up out of another mountain.

The character for **ride** or **sit** shows two people on benches.

Adding new strokes to characters gives them new meanings:

A **man, rén**

man   rén

stretching out his arms is **big, dà**.

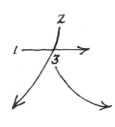

big   dà

A **tree, mù**

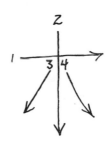

tree   mù

with **roots** showing is **běn**.

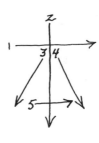

root   běn

Characters can be **combined** to make new words.

A **woman**, nǚ

 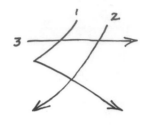

woman   **nǚ**

with a **child**, zǐ

 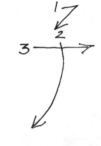

child   **zǐ**

means **good**, hǎo

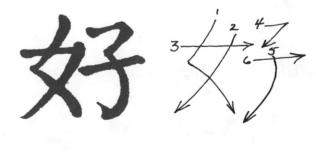

good   **hǎo**

Because in China — and everywhere — a mother with her child is a **good** thing.

An **ear**, **ĕr**

耳

ear   ĕr

at the **door**, **mén**

門

door   mén

means to **listen**, **wén**.

聞

listen   wén

A **mouth, kǒu**

mouth   **kǒu**

at the **door, mén**

door   **mén**

means **to ask for, wèn**.

to ask for   **wèn**

Notice that **wèn,** "to ask for," has a falling tone, but **wén,** "to listen," has a rising tone. Chinese has many, many words that sound the same except for the different tone.

Other characters can be used together to express new ideas without changing the Chinese words they represent.

 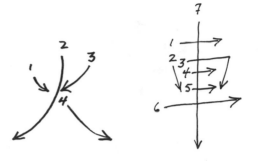

fire + **cart**   **huǒ** + **chē**

is a **train**.

A steam locomotive is a **cart** with **fire**.

 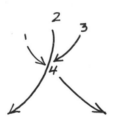 

fire + **mountain**   **huǒ** + **shān**

is a **volcano**.

A **volcano** is a **mountain** with **burning** rock.

Repeating the same character also makes a different word:

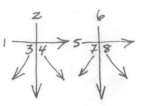

two trees   **forest**   **lín**

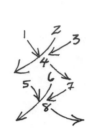

two fires   **blaze, burning**   **yán**

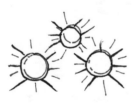

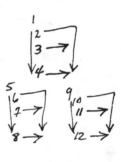

three suns   **crystal, clear**   **jīn**

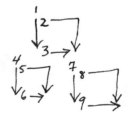

three mouths   **taste**   **pǐn**

The character for **language** combines

言 with 舌

話

| words | tongue | language | hùa |

The character for **vision** combines

ネ with 見

視

| spirit | to see | vision | shì |

The character for **lightning** also means **electricity**. It combines one character **above** another.

雨 over 田

| rain | field | add a streak of | **lightning** |

電

| electricity | diàn |

Although Chinese writing comes from very ancient times, new words can always be added for modern ideas and inventions.

Take the character for **electricity** that you just learned,

add the character for **language,**

electricity

language

and you have **telephone**.

電話

telephone
diàn hùa

To write **television,**
just add the character for
vision to **electricity.**

television
diàn shì

This wonderful group of characters means:
a giant general purpose transistorized digital computer

晶体管大型通用数字计算机

jīng   tǐ   quǎn   dà   xíng   tōng   yòng   shù   zì   jì   suàn   jī

Let's read and write a sentence in Chinese using characters and words that are in this book.

牛 羊 坐 火 車

Niú　　　　**yáng**　　　　**zuò**　　　　**huǒ**　　　　**chē**.

Look back through the book for meanings of any words you do not remember, and for the stroke order, before you write. Some short English words are "understood" in Chinese without being spoken or written. You will have to add "the" and "and" when you write the sentence in English. (Answer on last page.)

Are you surprised to discover that you can read and write Chinese, a language without an alphabet?

Many Chinese homes have frames or scrolls of **calligraphy** hanging on the walls. Fine writing, and the choice of a suitable text, is considered as much a fine art as painting and poetry.

The Chinese family pictured here has chosen a scroll which reads, "May all your goings-out and your comings-in be peaceful."

Banners, posters and cards carry good wishes for New Year celebrations, usually on red paper. Red is the color for good luck.

"May your happiness be as wide as the Eastern Sea."

"May you have peace and health in four seasons."

"Wishing you ten-thousand generations."

Chinese writing is used today by nearly **1,000,000,000 people** in China.

Japanese and Korean writing, developed from Chinese, is used by **160,000,000 more**.

You have just taken a giant step toward knowing **1,160,000,000 people** and their culture by **learning how they write**.

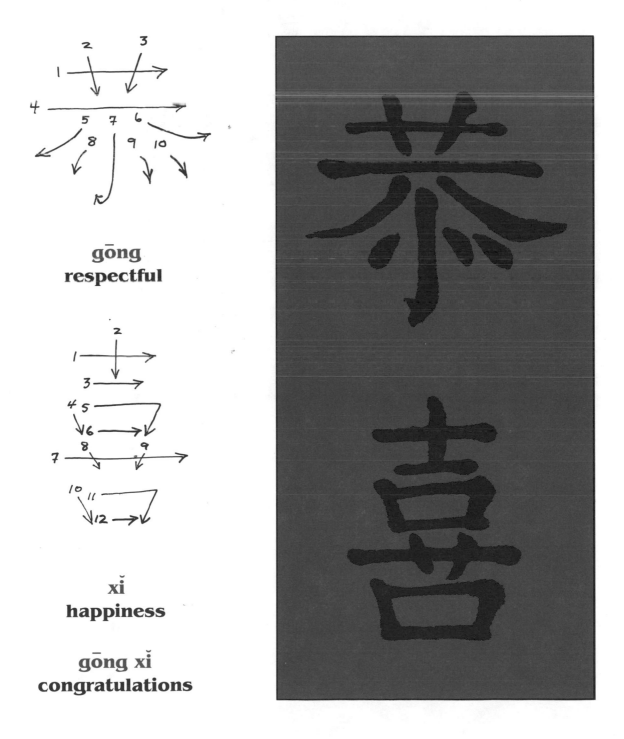

gōng
respectful

xǐ
happiness

gōng xǐ
congratulations

The ox and the sheep ride the train.

(Answer to question on page 27.)